ADVANC

In John Gosslee's debut collection, ᴵ², perfection sonnets that masterfully treat the characters of the western zodiac. Lyrically intense, each poem portrays a compelling portrait that breathes new life into an age-old celestial system. With a musician's heart, an eye for detail, and stunning craftsmanship, Gosslee explores the intricacies of the twelve signs — from Aries to Pisces — while dazzling the reader with his descriptive powers. These are illuminating and memorable poems from a new and authentic voice.

— Carolyn Kreiter-Foronda,
Poet Laureate of Virginia, 2006-2008

The poet John Gosslee has written a dozen sonnets, one for each astrological sign. His engagement with original patterns in a verse simultaneously free and formal, and containing a certain pervasive tone that might be described as gloomy frivolity, is entirely his own. To read these poems is to submerge oneself in a world of chance, change, and possibility, while never being allowed to forget the limits that reality, the reality of the self and of the literal, imposes on such notions as freedom or utopia ("The world of worlds portrayed in pastel blue"). Gosslee has suffused his verse with a particular humanity and an appreciation for the absurd, even the grotesque, while maintaining a quietly precise sense of modulation and an unerring gaze.
Though the rhymes and syntax are somewhat stilted at times, including some archaic contractions and inversions, the original, often startling imagery and rhythms carry the poems through. Some are epistolary,

others purely descriptive. All contain touches of exotica: temple domes, ruby pools, almond moonlight, violet blades. There is a medieval, almost Arthurian, quality running through many of the poems. One may find "poisonous vats and kegs," catacombs and even a martyr here. Notions of quest, hope, sacrifice and destiny abound. The sonnet with the most religious inference, "Virgo — The Virgin," is a supplication: "Queen of earth, preserver of mankind / Survey the ruin and rebuild our light." Elsewhere, a "lotus shrine" appears.

Yet, alongside crystals and jewels, we also find the commonplace "homemade loaf of bread…/ With a cup of coffee…" ("Pisces"). "Libra: Lady Justice" begins with these straightforward lines:

> My meetings with you have been quick and fleet
> From thought to meaning and plus to fraction

In orchestrating his poetics, Gosslee creates a tricky dialog between the human and the ideal, between what we can and what we can't control. He accomplishes this with a combination of spontaneity and clearheaded distillation. This is the kind of work that comes around rarely.

— Larry Fagin,
Professor of Poetics, New School University

12

Sonnets for the Zodiac

by John Gosslee

French Translation
by Elizabeth D. Watson

Spanish Translation
by Jose M. Guerrero

Gival Press

Arlington, Virginia

Published by Gival Press, an imprint of Gival Press, LLC.

For information please write:
Gival Press, LLC
P. O. Box 3812,
Arlington, VA 22203
www.givalpress.com

First edition

ISBN 978-1-92-8589-58-7
eISBN 978-1-92-8589-64-8
Library of Congress Control Number: 2011927144

Artwork Cover: "Los Signos del Zodiaco" by Juan Antonio Silva Galindo.
Photo of John Gosslee by Lauren Baker.
Design by Ken Schellenberg.

Acknowledgments:
Thank you to Spanish artist Juan Antonio Silva Galindo, to Nathan Susman who conceptualized the cover layout, to Chris Foley who edited the Spanish and French translations.

FOR AMANDA

ARIES

THE RAM'S BAA | ARIES

A red robed ram in pentacle flames,
Floats along cliff and mountain range, prancing
With a diamond skull and iron leg games
It protects itself by horn raised lancing;
Sirens for spirits through ram's hollow horn
Reach Aries sipping at a ruby pool:
Musicians drum on its kindred's skin torn
By a sacrifice o'er a mortal duel.

Their hands shake with experience and concern,
Siding with courage after hands withdraw,
Aries' sight observes vaguest terrors burn—
Marked by any errors in spoken law:
Encounters challenge and as well reveal
What intolerance attempts to conceal.

LE BÊLEMENT DU BÉLIER | ♈

Un bélier en habits rouges dans le pentacle de feu
Flotte au long de l'escarpement, caracolant,
Le crâne en losange, de ses pattes de fer jouant,
Il se protège, corne levée, perçant;
Des sirènes pour les âmes, à travers la corne creuse
Rejoignent le Bélier, buvant à une mare rubis:
Des musicians tambourinent sur la peau de ses
        semblables, dechirée
Par une sacrifice: résultat d'un duel mortel.

Leurs mains tremblent d'expérience et d'anxiété,
Se joignant au courage une fois les mains retirées,
Les yeux du Bélier regardent brûler les terreurs les plus
        floues —
Marquées par toute erreur dans la loi articulée:
Les rencontres défient et de plus révèlent
Ce que l'intolérance essaie de cacher.

ARIES | EL BAA DEL MORNECO

Un morneco enropado de rojo en llamas de pentáculo,
Flota por precipicio y cordillera montañosa, brincando,
Con una clavera de diamante y juegos de piernas de
     hierro,
Se protege con sus cuernos en alto lanzando;
El llamado a espiritus a travéz del cuerno vacío de
     morneco
Alcanza a Aries sorbeteando en un pozo rubí:
Músicos tamborean sobre el cuero de su familiar
     desgarrado
Por un sacrificio sobre un duelo mortal.

Sus manos tiemblan con experiencia y preocupación
Adheriéndose al coraje después del retiro de las manos,
La mira de Aries observa los más vagos terrores
     incendiarse—
Marcados por cualquier error de ley orada:
Confronta al desafío y asimismo revela
Lo que la intolerancia intenta cubrir.

AIRIES | ♈

21 March

22 March

23 March

24 March

25 March

26 March

27 March

28 March

28 March

29 March

30 March

31 March

1 April

2 April

3 April

4 April

5 April

6 April

7 April

8 April

9 April

10 April

11 April

12 April

13 April

14 April

15 April

16 April

17 April

18 April

19 April

20 April

TAURUS

BULLS ALWAYS CHARGE | TAURUS

The world of worlds portrayed in pastel blue
Hangs from the rafters of the temple dome,
I marvel at, bow to, this inner home —
And ask the copper Venus: please make true
Stout violet blades and topaz drops of dew,
To free us from this winding catacomb,
Whose exit we seek, while others still roam —
Puzzled by the passages we've been through.

I know what is here and what has commenced
The divine past cannot be dispensed!
Within work, I will reap the sweet future
And heal the devoted as a suture;
Observation alleviates wonder —
Then there is time to sow, plow, or blunder.

LA CHARGE DU TAUREAU | ♉

Si le monde des mondes dessiné en bleu pastel
Est suspendu aux poutres de la coupole du temple,
Je m'étonne, m'incline devant ce foyer intime
Et demande à la Vénus cuivrée: veuille rendre juste
De grosses feuilles violettes et gouttes de rosée topazes
Pour nous libérer des catacombes serpentées
Dont on cherche la sortie, alors que les autres errent
        encore —
Déconcertés par les corridors par lesquels nous sommes
        passés.

Je sais ce qui est là et ce qui a commencé
Le passé divin ne peut être rejeté!
C'est par le travail que je moissonerai le futur doux
Et guérirai les dévoués comme une suture;
L'observation calme l'émerveillement —
Alors il y a du temps pour semer, labourer ou gaffer.

LA CHARGE DU TAUREAU | ♉

El mundo de mundos pintado en azúl pastel
Guinda de las vigas de la cúpula del templo,
Yo admiro, me inclino, a esta casa interior —
Y le pido a la Venus cobre: Por favor has real
Robustas cuchillas moradas y gotas de rocío topacio,
Para liberarnos de esta sinuosa catacumba,
De la cual buscamos salida, mientras otros aún vagan —
Confundidos por los pasillos por los que hemos pasado.

Yo sé lo que hay aquí y lo que ha empezado
¡El divino pasado no puede ser dispensado!
En el trabajo, yo segaré el dulce porvenir
Y curaré los devotos como una sutura;
La observación alivia el asombro —
Así hay tiempo para segar, arar o errar.

TAURUS | ♉ | TAURO

21 April

22 April

23 April

24 April

25 April

26 April

27 April

28 April

28 April

29 April

30 April

1 May

2 May

3 May

4 May

5 May

6 May

7 May

8 May

9 May

10 May

11 May

12 May

13 May

14 May

15 May

16 May

17 May

18 May

19 May

20 May

GEMINI

THE TWINS OF SPRING | GEMINI

Hybrid mind, quicksilver comprehension,
Destined balancing four arms and four legs;
Movement is unlimited, while love begs
Mercury's still temperate dimension:
Divert unconscious states of dissension
And reflect on fortune above the rags,
While cracking the poisonous vats and kegs
That the lifeless drink from to lose tension.

May June award your life's sacrifices well
And Spring place you in burgeoning orchard;
We would not be — without your providence;
Look through the vale until differences tell
The reasons for the peaceful and tortured,
Then, please, take us into your confidence.

LES GÉMEAUX DU PRINTEMPS | ♊

L'esprit hybride, la connaissance vif-argentée,
Destinés à équilibrer quatre bras, quatre jambes;
Le mouvement est sans limites, tandis que l'amour
    supplie
La dimension toujours modérée de Mercure:
Détourne les états inconscients de dissension
Et médite sur la fortune au-delà des haillons,
Tout en craquant les cuves et caques empoisonnées
Où boivent les inanimés pour perdre la tension.

Que juin t'accorde bien les sacrifices de la vie
Et que le printemps te place dans le verger en fleurs;
Nous ne serions pas vivants — sans ta providence;
Regarde au-delà de la vallée jusqu'à ce que les différences
Révèlent les raisons pour les paisibles et torturés,
Et alors, de grâce, confie-toi à nous.

GEMINIS | LOS GEMELOS DE PRIMAVERA

Mente híbrida, comprensión de mercurio,
Destinado balanceando cuatro brasos y cuatro piernas;
Movimiento ilimitado, mientras el amor suplica
Dimensión de Mercurio aún atemperado:
Desvia estados inconscientes de discordia
Y refleja sobre la fortuna encima de los harapos,
Mientras cruje los tanques y barriles venenosos
De los cuales los fallecidos beben para disipar la tensión

Que Junio te otorge bien los sacrificios de tu vida
Y que la Primavera te ponga en huerta floreciente;
No pudiéramos existir — sin tú provición;
Mira a través del valle hasta que las diferencias
    divulguen
Las razones para los pacíficos y torturados,
Luego, por favor, tomanos en tu confianza.

GEMINI | ♊ | GEMINIS

21 May

22 May

23 May

24 May

25 May

26 May

27 May

28 May

28 May

29 May

30 May

31 May

1 June

2 June

3 June

4 June

5 June

6 June

7 June

8 June

9 June

10 June

11 June

12 June

13 June

14 June

15 June

16 June

17 June

18 June

19 June

20 June

CANCER

THE CRAB'S PRESENT | CANCER

Crawling on the bottom becomes tiring,
Retreat to the isle of the lotus shrine,
Where the turtle and the sphinx are aspiring —
Drunk on your almond-moonlight's amber wine;
Drift there on the chariot like currents,
Traipse over the pearl and yellow-glass beach —
An indigo door waits with assurance!
Drag through it an orange — fallen for each.

The innate will of being a martyr
Is chiseled on your compassionate heart,
But if able to buy, deal, or barter
With destiny — you will have done your part.
You offered us breath and now we flower
Into laudable tendrils for each hour.

LE CADEAU DU CANCER | ♋

Se traînant sur le fond devient fatigant,
Retire-toi dans l'île du sanctuaire du lotus,
Où la tortue et le sphinx aspirent —
Ivres du vin ambré de ton clair de lune amande;
Dérive là-bas à bord du chariot comme les courants,
Ballade-toi sur le sable de perles et de verre jaune —
Une porte azurés t'attend avec assurance!
Fais-y traîner une orange — tombée pour chacun.

La volonté innée de la vie de martyr
Est ciselée sur ton coeur compatissant,
Mais si tu es capable d'acheter, négocier ou troquer
Avec le destin, tu auras fait ta part.
Tu nous donnas le souffle et donc on s'épanouit
Devenant des vrilles dignes de louanges pour chaque
      heure.

CANCER | EL PRESENTE DEL CANGREJO

Raptor en el fondo se hace fatigoso.
Retirese a la isla del santuario del loto,
Donde la tortuga y la esfinge están aspirando—
Embriagadas con el vino ambar de tu luz de luna
    almendra.
Derivado hacia allá sobre las corrientes como carrozas,
Anda penosamente sobre la playa de perla y vidrio
    amarillo—
¡Una puerta índigo espera con garantía!
Arrastra a travéz de ella una naranja—caída para cada
    uno.

El deseo innato de ser un mártir
Está tallado en tu corazón compasionado
Pero si logras comprar, acordar o trocar,
Con el destino—habrás hecho tu parte.
Nos has ofrecido aliento y ahora florecemos
En zarcillos loables por cada hora.

CANCER | ♋

21 June

22 June

23 June

24 June

25 June

26 June

27 June

28 June

28 June

29 June

30 June

1 July

2 July

3 July

4 July

5 July

6 July

7 July

8 July

9 July

10 July

11 July

12 July

13 July

14 July

15 July

16 July

17 July

18 July

19 July

20 July

21 July

22 July

LEO

SUMMER'S ROAR | LEO

Age permits sunflowers in heather-field,
Where sprawled the lion coaxes sweet laurel —
Into nostrils that detect scent's floral
Next to nearby prey — searching for a shield.
Cat's eye fixes and refuses to yield.
Compelled by blood and animal chorale:
Self-preservation is simply moral
When claw and fangs are the weapons to wield.

When I was cornered you defended me
And persevered to teach me what you knew,
But the Sun shines on every soul being —
And that is why the galaxies pursue
Recollections of reflections, seeing
That creating entities remain free.

LES LIONS PRINTANIERS | ♌

L'âge admet des tournesols dans le champ de bruyère,
Où, étendu, le lion invite le laurier doux —
À entrer dans les narines, découvrant des fleurs
        parfumées
À côté de la proie voisine — cherchant quelque sécurité.
L'oeil du chat se fixe and refuse de fléchir.
Poussé par le sang et le choeur d'animaux:
L'instinct de conservation est simplement moral
Lorsque griffes et canines sont les armes à brandir.

Quand je fus en difficulté tu me défendis
Et persévéras pour m'apprendre ce que tu savais,
Mais le soleil brille sur toute âme vivante —
Et c'est pourquoi les galaxies poursuivent
Des souvenirs des réflexions, assurant
Que la création d'êtres reste libre.

LEO | LOS LEONES DE PRIMAVERA

La edad permite las girasoles en campos de brezo,
Donde el león despatarrado embauca dulce laurel —
A su nariz que detecta un floreado de olores
Al lado de caza cercana — buscando un escudo.
El ojo felino se fija y rechaza ceder.
Compelado por sangre y coro animal:
La preservación propia es simplemente moral
Cuando las garras y colmillos son las armas que esgrimir.

Cuando estuve acorralado me defendiste
Y te empeñaste en enseñarme lo que sabías,
Pero el Sol brilla en cada ser espiritual —
Y eso es porque las galaxias buscan
Recuerdos de reflejos, viendo
Que las entidades creadoras permanecen libres.

LEO | ฦ

23 July

24 July

25 July

26 July

27 July

28 July

28 July

29 July

30 July

31 July

1 August

2 August

3 August

4 August

5 August

6 August

7 August

8 August

9 August

10 August

11 August

12 August

13 August

14 August

15 August

16 August

17 August

18 August

19 August

20 August

21 August

22 August

23 August

VIRGO

THE VIRGIN | VIRGO

Queen of earth, preserver of mankind,
Survey the ruin and rebuild our light:
That tone aggravation's dustiest sight
Which can only see clearly as rain's bind.
When destiny's ancient faces are lined —
Immortal lake forest ruins are quite
The gothic hot-bubbling springs at night,
With an opal glow surrounding, refined.

All grace, propriety, and health are yours:
The finest cuisine on palatial grounds,
Prepared by chefs, presented with servant's love,
Are a few of the honors from the scores
Of admirers orchestrated in bounds,
To you, the only one always above.

LA VIERGE | ♍

Reine de la terre, conservatrice de l'humanité,
Surveille les ruines et reconstruis notre lumière:
Ce ton, le plus poussiéreux spectacle de l'ennui,
Qui ne comprend clairement que comme lien de la pluie.
Quand les visages anciens du sort sont ridés —
Les ruines immortelles de la forêt lacustre deviennent
De véritables eaux gothiques, chaudes et pétillantes la
      nuit,
Avec une lueur opale tout autour, épurée.

Toute la grâce, les bienséances, et la santé sont à toi:
La cuisine la plus raffinée dans le parc magnifique,
Préparée par des chefs, présentée avec l'amour d'un
      serviteur,
N'est qu'une partie des honneurs de la foule
D'admirateurs orchestrés sans bornes,
Pour toi, la seule toujours là-haut.

VIRGO | LA VIRGEN

Reina de la tierra, preservadora de la humanidad,
Examina la ruina y reconstruye nuestra luz:
Que entinta la vista más polvorosa de la agravación
Que sólo puede ver claramente como el amarro de la
    lluvia.
Cuando las caras ancianas del destino están rayadas—
Ruinas forestales inmortales del lago son totalmente
Fuentes termales góticas burbujeantes de noche,
Con un lustro ópalo velando, refinado.

Toda gracia, decencia y salud son tuyas;
La cocina más fina del palacio.
Preparada por chefs, presentado con el amor de
    sirvientes,
Son pocos de los honores de los montones
De admiradores orquestrados atados,
A ti, el único siempre más allá de todo.

VIRGO | ♍

24 August

25 August

26 August

27 August

28 August

28 August

29 August

30 August

31 August

1 September

2 September

3 September

4 September

5 September

6 September

7 September

8 September

9 September

10 September

11 September

12 September

13 September

14 September

15 September

16 September

17 September

18 September

19 September

20 September

21 September

22 September

LIBRA

LADY JUSTICE | LIBRA

My meetings with you have been quick and fleet
From thought to meaning and plus to fraction;
Is life fair in an hour's interaction?
You, bestow desires or passions deplete,
And decide from the start, but are discreet,
Allowing judgments to change through action—
By disavowing outside distraction.
The scales are above any that compete;

A clear open space rejuvenates you;
Air is the slow breath of death, so you live
Enveloped in the earth—and free for fire;
Writhe tornado and balance with your clue—
That which wouldn't transcend the worldly sieve,
Or simply rework your method's attire.

MADAME LA BALANCE | ♎

Mes rencontres avec toi furent brèves et fugitives
De l'idée jusqu'à la signifiance et de plus à la fraction;
La vie est-elle juste en une heure d'entretien?
Toi, tu accordes les désirs ou épuises les passions,
Et décides dès le départ, mais avec discrétion,
Permettant que les jugements changent par l'action —
En désavouant la distraction extérieure.
À tout ce qui te fait concurrence, tu es supérieure;

Un espace ouvert et clair te rajeunit;
L'air est l'haleine lente de la mort, alors tu vis
Enveloppée dans la terre — et libre au feu;
Tords-toi tornade et équilibre-toi avec ton signe —
Ce qui ne transcenderait pas la passoire temporelle,
Ou refais simplement le revêtement de ta méthode.

LIBRA | DAMA JUSTICIA

Mis encuentros contigo han sido rápidos y fugaces
De pensamiento a significado y suma a fracción;
¿Es la vida justa en una hora de interacción?
Tú, otorga deseos y pasiones agotadas,
Y decide desde el principio, pero siendo discreta,
Permitiendo el cambio a jucios a travéz de la acción —
Repudiando la distracción externa
La balanza guinda sobre cualquiera que compite;

Un espacio claro y abierto te rejuvence;
El aire es el aliento lento de la muerte, así que vives
Envuelto en la tierra — y libre para fuego;
Tornado retorciendo y balanceando con tu pista —
Eso que no superaría más allá del harnero mundano,
O simplemente reproduce la vestimenta de tu método.

LIBRA | ♎

23 September

24 September

25 September

26 September

27 September

28 September

28 September

29 September

30 September

1 October

2 October

3 October

4 October

5 October

6 October

7 October

8 October

9 October

10 October

11 October

12 October

13 October

14 October

15 October

16 October

17 October

18 October

19 October

20 October

21 October

22 October

23 October

SCORPIO

METAMORPHOSIS | SCORPIO

Leaving the soft eggs, drinking the aloe,
Then scurrying back to the laden nest —
Long protected for their unbeknownst quest,
That you are on, preparing our tallow;
Stinging is greater than the snake's swallow —
That the scavengers view erroneous;
Tail pierces each unsanctimonious
Being that chooses to closely follow;

In oceans are comrades in many schools,
But you have become trapped under thick glass;
Sunlight at noon will destroy your swift form,
And as your skeleton's smoke gently spools,
It's inhaled by a vulture that will pass
Over forest fires, phoenixes swarm.

LA MÉTAMORPHOSE DU SCORPION |
♏

Laissant les oeufs mous, buvant de l'aloès,
Puis détalant au nid chargé —
Protégés longtemps à cause de leur quête inconnue
Que tu poursuis, en préparant notre chandelle;
Ta piqûre est pire que d'être avalé par un serpent —
Que les pilleurs jugent erroné;
Ta queue perce chaque être non-moralisateur
Qui choisit de te suivre de près;

Des camarades marines se trouvent dans des bancs
     divers,
Mais tu es piégé sous un verre épais;
À midi l''ensoleillement détruira ta forme fine,
Et alors que la fumée de ton squelette se bobine
Doucement, elle est inhalée par un vautour qui passera
Par-dessus les feux de forêts, des phénixs s'agglutinent.

ESCORPIÓN | LA METAMÓRFOSIS DEL ALACRÁN

Dejando los huevos blandos, tomando el aloe
luego correteando devuelta al nido cargado —
protegido lánguidamente para su misión ignorada,
en la que estás, preparando nuestro sebo;
La picadura, superior al engullo de vibora-
lo que los carroñeros ven erróneo;
la cola penetra cada ser desvergonzado
que escoge seguir de cerca;

Er mares hay camaradas juntadas en muchas escuelas,
pero tú te has vuelto prisionero debajo del cristal grueso;
la luz del sol a mediodía destrozara tu forma ágil,
y mientras se esfuma lentamente el humo de tu esqueleto,
es inhalado por un buitre que pasará
sobre incendios forestales, donde se reunen los fénix.

SCORPIO | ♏ | ESCORPIÓN

24 October

25 October

26 October

27 October

28 October

28 October

29 October

30 October

31 October

1 November

2 November

3 November

4 November

5 November

6 November

7 November

8 November

9 November

10 November

11 November

12 November

13 November

14 November

15 November

16 November

17 November

18 November

19 November

20 November

21 November

22 November

SAGITTARIUS

THE CENTAUR'S DUALITY | SAGITTARIUS

She picked him from among men around her,
Youth no doubt played the first role in her choice;
Selflessness, her only motive and voice
Knew his potential, she made an offer:
Indulgence changes archer to cougar.
Showered with money, drugs and most decoys,
He shunned opportunity for the ploys
Of degenerative waves in a blur.

On the west coast she lies in the sunlight—
Altering her form for education,
He seeks, having knowledge's neutral sight,
Making names for the future's great nation,
Jupiter and Neptune will be the dawn,
Helping two lovers like a dragon.

LE SAGITTAIRE : LA DUALITÉ DU CENTAURE | ⟿

Elle le choisit parmi des hommes qui l'entouraient,
La jeunesse sans doute joua le premier rôle dans son
       choix;
Le désintéressement, son seul moyen et sa seule voix
Reconnut sa promesse, elle fit une offre:
L'indulgence change l'archer en couguar.
Comblé d'argent, de droques et de la plupart des leurres,
Il fuit l'opportunité et embrassa les stratagèmes
Des vagues dégénératives en masse confuse.

Sur la côte-ouest elle s'allonge sous le soleil—
Changeant de forme au nom de l'éducation,
Lui, il cherche, ayant le regard neutre de la connaissance,
Créant des noms pour l'avenir de la grande nation,
Jupiter et Neptune seront l'aube,
Aidant les deux amants comme un dragon.

SAGITARIO | LA DUALIDAD DEL CENTAURO

Ella lo escogió de los hombres alrededor de ella,
La juventud, sin duda, jugó el primer papel en su
　　　elección;
El altruismo, su único motivo y voz
Conocía su potencial, y le hizo una oferta;
La tolerancia cambia al arquero a puma;
Colmado de dinero, drogas y la mayoría de señuelos,
Él rechazó la oportunidad por artimañas
De olas degenerativas nebulosas.

En la costa oeste ella reposa en la luz del sol—
Alterando su forma para la educación,
Él busca, teniendo la vista neutral del conocimiento,
Haciendo nombres para la nación futura grandiosa,
Jupiter y Neptuno serán el amanecer,
Ayudando a dos amantes como un dragón.

SAGITTARIUS | ⛢ | SAGITARIO

23 November

24 November

25 November

26 November

27 November

28 November

28 November

29 November

30 November

1 December

2 December

3 December

4 December

5 December

6 December

7 December

8 December

9 December

10 December

11 December

12 December

13 December

14 December

15 December

16 December

17 December

18 December

19 December

20 December

21 December

CAPRICORN

THE GOAT'S YOKE | CAPRICORN

Accustomed to the night's vacant bedroom—
We met and ruled the streets, as you looked faster
For remedies to psychic disaster,
I watched you change thoughts in diachronic boom!
Enchanted with telepathic heirloom,
Passed abruptly to you, somehow master
The technique of controlling the plaster
That the artists of all domains will groom.

Now words were unspoken. We represent
What cannot be said, remember the last
Thought you could not, resting is for a god.
Eat inclinations food, look at crescent
Moons and eyes plotting like architects past
Limits with compassion's contagious rod

LE CAPRICORNE : LE JOUG DE LA CHÈVRE | ♑

Accoutumé à la chambre vide de la nuit—
Au rendez-vous nous régnâmes sur les rues, alors que tu cherchais
    tu cherchais
Plus vivement des remèdes aux désastres psychiques,
Je te regardai changer d'idées avec un essor diachronique!
Enchanté de l'héritage télépathique,
Brusquement légué à toi, tu maîtrises d'une certaine
    façon
La technique pour modeler le plâtre
Que les artistes de tous domaines prépareront.
Maintenant les mots restent tacites. On représente
Ce qui ne se dit pas, rappelle-toi la dernière pensée
Que tu ne pourrais pas exprimer, le repos est pour les
    dieux.
Mange de nourrissantes tendances, regarde les lunes
Croissantes et les yeux complotant comme les architectes
    d'antan
Les limites, avec la baguette contagieuse de la
    compassion.

CAPRICORNIO | EL YUGO DE LA CABRA

Acostumbrado al dormitorio vacío de la noche —
Nos reuníamos y dominábamos las calles, mientras
     buscabas aún más rápidamente
Remedios para desastres psíquicos,
¡Te observé cambiar de pensamiento en auge diacrónico!
Encantado por una reliquia telepática,
Pasado abruptamente a tí, de alguna manera superar
La técnica de controlar el yeso
Que los artistas de todos los dominios prepararán.

Ahora las palabras fueron tácitas. Representamos
Lo que no se puede decir, recuerda el último
Pensamiento que no podías, descansar es para un dios.
Come el alimento de la inclinación, mira las lunas
Crecientes y ojos tramando como arquitectos más allá
De los límites con la vara contagiosa de la compasión.

CAPRICORN | ♑ | CAPRICORNIO

22 December

23 December

24 December

25 December

26 December

27 December

28 December

28 December

29 December

30 December

31 December

1 January

2 January

3 January

4 January

5 January

6 January

7 January

8 January

9 January

10 January

11 January

12 January

13 January

14 January

15 January

16 January

17 January

18 January

19 January

AQUARIUS

THE WATER BEARER | AQUARIUS

In the distance flint sparks, tonight feels chilled —
As the tender winter evening we spent
Conversing about our histories lent
To us, and aspirations now fulfilled.
The seeds we cast and planted on land tilled
Still surrender foliage, season sent;
Designs of a billion stars, in extent
Covered our fields, engraved by the wheel willed.

Recording, oh so carefully, you saw,
The power in sound when mixed with light.
We do not have to wait a hundred years
To plant fruit bearing trees in springtime's thaw,
Along public sidewalks for our delight,
Opening choices for others and peers.

LE VERSEAU | ≈

De loin le silex jette des étincelles, ce soir est gelé —
Nous passâmes la soirée tendre de l'hiver
Parlant des histoires prêtées
À nous, et des aspirations maintenant réalisées.
Les graines que nous avions semées et plantées sur la
      terre labourée
Encore cèdent leur feuillage, par la saison envoyé;
Les dessins d'un milliard d'étoiles, dans une mesure
Couvrirent nos champs, gravés par la roue désirée.

Enregistrant, si soignesusement, tu constatas
Le pouvoir du son mêlé avec la lumière.
On ne doit pas attendre cent ans
Pour planter des arbres fruitiers au dégel
Le long de trottoirs publics pour notre joie,
Ouvrant aux autres et aux pairs des choix.

ACUARIO | EL CARGADOR DE AGUA

En la distancia chispea el sílex, esta noche se siente fría —
Como la noche tierna de invierno que pasamos
Conversando de nuestros cuentos que
Nos prestaron y nuestras aspiraciones ya realisadas.
Las semillas que echamos y plantamos en la tierra cultivada
Aun rinden follaje, enviados por la temporada;
Diseños de un billón de estrellas, en amplitud
Cubrieron nuestros campos, imprimidos por las ruedas intencionadas.

Grabando, ¡oh! tan cuidadosamente, tú viste,
El poder en el sonido al ser mezclado con luz,
No tenemos que esperar cien años
Para plantar árboles frutales en el derretir de la primavera.
A lo largo de veredas públicas para nuestro placer,
Abriéndole opciones a otros y compañeros.

AQUARIUS | ♒ | ACUARIO

20 January

21 January

22 January

23 January

24 January

25 January

26 January

27 January

28 January

28 January

29 January

30 January

31 January

1 February

2 February

3 February

4 February

5 February

6 February

7 February

8 February

9 February

10 February

11 February

12 February

13 February

14 February

15 February

16 February

17 February

18 February

19 February

PISCES

TWO FISH | PISCES

Intuition rips into each old day;
With amethyst eyes and golden physique
Ahead of my lifetime and of this week,
Remembering from webbed paws — the true way,
I mapped before hands with circular claws,
Crystal, jeweled, and stone references,
That show my path without preferences
And enlarge laughter, through these ancient flaws.

A homemade loaf of bread is always good,
With a cup of coffee shared by a friend,
As we stand where we have longingly stood —
In graces of the highest spirit's end;
We know everything is a passing fad
And make all listen to destiny clad.

LES DEUX POISSONS | ⦿⦿

L'intuition fend chaque jour passé;
Avec les yeux améthystes and le physique doré
En avance sur mon vivant et sur cette semaine,
Se rappelant par des pattes palmées — la piste vraie,
Je dressai la carte, les mains aux griffes circulaires,
Des références de cristal, bijou et pierre,
Qui démontrent ma voie sans préférences
Et intensifient le rire par ces fautes anciennes.

Un pain fait maison est toujours bon,
Avec une tasse de café partagée avec un ami,
Voilà on se tient debout là où on se tenait avec
    convoitise —
Dans les grâces de la fin du plus haut esprit;
On sait que tout est une folie passagère
Qui s'éteint
Et fait écouter à tout le monde le sort revêtu.

PISCIS | LOS DOS PECES

La intuición rasga dentro de cada viejo día;
Con ojos amatista y físico dorado
Adelantado de mi época y de esta semana,
Recordando desde las garras palmeadas—el camino
    verdadero,
Tracé frente a manos con garras circulares,
Referencias cristales, ajoyadas y de piedra,
Que indican mi vereda sin preferencias,
Y amplian risas a través de estas faltas antiguas.

Una barra de pan casero siempre va bien,
Con una taza de café compartida con un amigo,
Mientras nos paramos donde nos hemos parado
    anhelando—
En las gracias del final del espíritu más alto;
Sabemos que todo es una manía pasajera
Y hacemos que todos escuchen la cubierta del destino.

PISCES | ♓ | PISCIS

20 February

21 February

22 February

23 February

24 February

25 February

26 February

27 February

28 February

28 February

29 February

1 March

2 March

3 March

4 March

5 March

6 March

7 March

8 March

9 March

10 March

11 March

12 March

13 March

14 March

15 March

16 March

17 March

18 March

19 March

20 March

More Poetry from Gival Press

Adamah: Poème by Céline Zins; translation by Peter Schulman

ISBN 13: 978-1-928589-46-4, $15.00
2010 Honorable Mention—Paris Book Festival for Poetry
This bilingual (French/English) collection by an eminent French poet/
writer is adeptly translated in this premiere edition.

Bones Washed With Wine: *Flint Shards from Sussex* and *Bliss*
by Jeff Mann

ISBN 13: 978-1-928589-14-3, $15.00
Includes the 1999 Gival Press Poetry Award winning collection. Jeff Mann
is "a poet to treasure both for the wealth of his language and the generosity
of his spirit."
—Edward Falco, author of *Acid*

Canciones para sola cuerda / Songs for a Single String
by Jesús Gardea; English translation by Robert L. Giron

ISBN 13: 978-1-928589-09-9, $15.00
Finalist for the 2003 Violet Crown Book Award—Literary Prose &
Poetry.
Love poems, with echoes of Neruda à la Mexicana, Gardea writes about
the primeval quest for the perfect woman.

Dervish by Gerard Wozek

ISBN 13: 978-1-928589-11-2, $15.00
Winner of the 2000 Gival Press Poetry Award / Finalist for the 2002
Violet Crown Book Award—Literary Prose & Poetry.
"By jove, these poems shimmer."
—Gerry Gomez Pearlberg, author of *Mr. Bluebird*

The Great Canopy by Paula Goldman

ISBN 13: 978-1-928589-31-0, $15.00
Winner of the 2004 Gival Press Poetry Award / 2006 Independent
Publisher Book Award—Honorable Mention for Poetry
"Under this canopy we experience the physicality of the body through
Goldman's wonderfully muscular verse as well the analytics of a mind that
tackles the meaning of Orpheus or the notion of desire."
—Richard Jackson, author of *Half Lives*

Honey by Richard Carr

ISBN 13: 978-1-928589-45-7, $15.00
Winner of the 2007 Gival Press Poetry Award / 2008 Finalist—ForeWord Magazine Book Award for Poetry
"*Honey* is a tour de force. Comprised of 100 electrifying microsonnets . . . The whole sequence creates a narrative that becomes, like the Hapax Legomenon, a form that occurs only once in a literature."
—Barbara Louise Ungar, author of *The Origin of the Milky Way*

Let Orpheus Take Your Hand by George Klawitter

ISBN 13: 978-1-928589-16-7, $15.00
Winner of the 2001 Gival Press Poetry Award
A thought provoking work that mixes the spiritual with stealthy desire, with Orpheus leading us out of the pit.

Metamorphosis of the Serpent God by Robert L. Giron

ISBN 13: 978-1-928589-07-5, $12.00
This collection "…embraces the past and the present, ethnic and sexual identity, themes both mythical and personal."
—*The Midwest Book Review*

Museum of False Starts by Chip Livingston

ISBN 13: 978-1-928589-49-5, $15.00
Livingston - a "mixed blood" poet - presents a new approach to poetry through his experience.
"…Chip Livingston makes the ordinary exotic, erotic and extraordinary."—Ai

On the Altar of Greece by Donna J. Gelagotis Lee

ISBN 13: 978-1-92-8589-36-5, $15.00
Winner of the 2005 Gival Press Poetry Award / 2007 Eric Hoffer Book Award: Notable for Art Category
"…*On the Altar of Greece* is like a good travel guide: it transforms reader into visitor and nearly into resident. It takes the visitor to the authentic places that few tourists find, places delightful yet still surprising, safe yet unexpected…."
—by Simmons B. Buntin, editor of *Terrain.org Blog*

On the Tongue by Jeff Mann

ISBN 13: 978-1-928589-35-8, $15.00
"…These poems are …nothing short of extraordinary."
—Trebor Healey, author of *Sweet Son of Pan*

The Nature Sonnets by Jill Williams

ISBN 13: 978-1-928589-10-5, $8.95
An innovative collection of sonnets that speaks to the cycle of nature and
life, crafted with wit and clarity. "Refreshing and pleasing."
—Miles David Moore, author of *The Bears of Paris*

The Origin of the Milky Way by Barbara Louise Ungar

ISBN 13: 978-1-928589-39-6, $15.00
Winner of the 2006 Gival Press Poetry Award / 2007 Adirondack Literary
Award for the Best Book of Poetry / 2008 Eric Hoffer Award—Notable
for Poetry / Silver 2008 Independent Publisher Book Award for Poetry
"…a fearless, unflinching collection about birth and motherhood, the
transformation of bodies. Ungar's poems are honestly brutal, candidly
tender. Their primal immediacy and intense intimacy are realized through
her dazzling sense of craft. Ungar delivers a wonderful, sensuous, visceral
poetry." —Denise Duhamel

Poetic Voices Without Borders edited by Robert L. Giron

ISBN 13: 978-1-928589-30-3, $20.00
2006 Writer's Notes Magazine Book Award—Notable for Art / 2006
Independent Publisher Book Award—Honorable Mention for Anthology
An international anthology of poetry in English, French, and Spanish,
including work by Grace Cavalieri, Jewell Gomez, Joy Harjo, Peter
Klappert, Jaime Manrique, C.M. Mayo, E. Ethelbert Miller, Richard
Peabody, Myra Sklarew and many others.

Poetic Voices Without Borders 2, edited by Robert L. Giron

ISBN 13: 978-1-928589-43-3, $20.00
Winner 2009 National Best Book Award for Anthologies / Runner-Up
2009 London Book Festival Award for Poetry / 2009 San Francisco Book
Festival—Honorable Mention for Poetry. Featuring poets Grace Cavalieri,
Rita Dove, Dana Gioia, Joy Harjo, Peter Klappert, Philip Levine, Gloria
Vando, and many other fine poets in English, French, and Spanish.

Prosody in England and Elsewhere:
A Comparative Approach by Leonardo Malcovati

ISBN 13: 978-1-928589-26-6, $20.00
The perfect tool for the poet but written for a non-specialist audience.

Tickets to a Closing Play by Janet I. Buck

ISBN 13: 978-1-928589-25-9, $15.00
Winner of the 2002 Gival Press Poetry Award
"…this rich and vibrant collection of poetry [is] not only serious and insightful, but a sheer delight to read."
—Jane Butkin Roth, editor of *We Used to Be Wives: Divorce Unveiled Through Poetry*

Voyeur by Rich Murphy

ISBN 13: 978-1-928589-48-8, $15.00
Winner of the 2008 Gival Press Poetry Award
"*Voyeur* is a work of vision and virtuosity. Concerned with relationships, marriage, sex and power, the poetry is dense, rapid, dazzling, the voice commanding, the speaker charismatic…spectacular."
—Richard Carr

Where a Poet Ought Not / Où c'qui faut pas by G. Tod Slone
(in English and French)

ISBN 13: 978-1-928589-42-6, $15.00
Poems inspired by French poets Léo Ferré and François Villon and the Québec poet Raymond Lévesque in what Slone characterizes as a need to speak up. "In other words, a poet should speak the truth as he sees it and fight his damnedest to overcome all the forces encouraging not to."

For a list of poetry published by Gival Press, please visit: *www.givalpress.com*

Books available via BookMasters, Ingram, the Internet, and other outlets.

Or Write:

Gival Press, LLC
PO Box 3812
Arlington, VA 22203
703.351.0079

Made in the USA
Charleston, SC
24 September 2011